D0119907

ENGLAND
Land of Legends

SELECT
EDITIONS

ENGLAND
Land of Legends

Alex Hook

SELECT
EDITIONS

Published 2004 in the UK exclusively for

SELECTABOOK
Folly road,
Roundway,
Devises,
Wiltshire
SN10 2HT

All enquiries please email selectabookltd@tiscali.co.uk

Copyright ©2004 Taj Books Ltd

Copyright under International, Pan American, and Universal Copyright Conventions. All rights reserved. No part of this book may be reproduced or transmitted in any form or by any means, electronic or mechanical, including photocopying, recording, or by any information storage-and-retrieval system, without written permission from the copyright holder. Brief passages (not to exceed 1,000 words) may be qouted for reviews.

All notations of errors or omissions (author inquiries, permissions) concerning the content of this book should be addressed to TAJ Books 27, Ferndown Gardens, Cobham, Surrey, UK, KT11 2BH, info@tajbooks.com.

ISBN 1-84406-031-4

Printed in China.
1 2 3 4 5 08 07 06 05 04

LONDON 8

SOUTHERN ENGLAND 22

EASTERN ENGLAND 60

MIDLANDS 68

THE NORTH 88

Introduction

With the rise of the Roman Empire it was only a matter of time before Rome decided to take Britain for themselves. Julius Caesar famously arrived in 55 and 54BC but returned to Gaul both times. In AD43 the Emperor Claudius sent four legions to conquer Britain, extending their influence to all but the fringes of the islands. They built a backbone of roads linking their cities across the country all the way north to almost the borders of Scotland where they built Hadrian's Wall (started in AD12), and then later and further north the Antonine Wall (c.AD140). Enough of Hadrian's Wall remains to give a flavour of this outpost of empire. The Romans stayed in Britain until the fifth century AD. Roman villas and temples as well as much smaller artefacts are continuously found across all the parts of the country settled by the Romans. When the Romans left central rule disappeared and the native Britons were left to fend for themselves against successive waves of invading Angles, Saxons, and Vikings tempted from the Continent by the rich pickings in Britain. The country was an ever-shifting matrix of small kingdoms, fiefdoms, and political alliances when Norman Duke William used his military might to enforce his rule after winning the Battle of Hastings in 1066. He started a hugely unpopular rule that left an impressive legacy of castles and cathedrals across the country. One of the most famous of these is the Tower of London, impressive today, it was an awesome symbol of the implacable might of the Norman Invasion to the subjugated Anglo-Saxons.

The Normans codified and regulated their new lands and compiled the great Domesday Book, a detailed record of all their feudal holdings and all the taxes due to them. England became a unified country for the first time since the Romans left 600 years earlier. Once established in England, they moved to take control of Wales and Ireland taking all possible lands into their tight feudal fists. Under the Norman kings was established a powerful aristocracy inextricably bound by feudal vows of loyalty and obedience who in turn ruled an underclass of Anglo Saxons. In time the power of the barons rebounded on the monarchy when King John was forced to sign the Magna Carta in June 1215 at Runnymede, conceding rights and privileges to his subjects and limitations on royal power. After many years of border wars England and Wales were united by the Statute of Rhuddlan, proclaimed by Edward I in 1284. This set up colonial government institutions for the Principality of Wales. From then on the monarch's oldest son and successor was invested as the Prince of Wales with lands and privileges of his own. In 1485 a man of Welsh descent, Henry Tudor, would be crowned Henry VII. During the age of the Tudors England assumed a previously unmatched importance in Europe in political, cultural, and artistic terms. Under King Henry VIII the religious complexion of the country was changed when he renounced the Roman Catholic church in favour of Protestantism. During this period all the abbeys and monasteries were dissolved and many of the buildings destroyed. However, many romantic ruins still remain around the country, such as Glastonbury, Fountains and Riveaux. Another significant advance in this period was the exploration across the Atlantic to the New World. The first colonies in north America failed, but slowly and surely settlements succeeded and a whole new world began. In August 1620 some religious dissenters left Southampton dock on the Mayflower, intent on finding a new life free from the established church. They had to put in for repairs at Plymouth before embarking on the long Atlantic crossing, to land at Plymouth Rock, in the land that would later become known as Massachusetts. They were not the first settlers in the New World, but they are the most famous. The greatest of the Tudors was Elizabeth I who left a strong and well-governed country to her cousin, King James VI of Scotland. Thus were the thrones of the two countries united as James VI became King James I of England, the first of the Stuart dynasty.

The Act of Union a century later in 1707 gave political permanence to this and Great Britain came into being. Like their ancestors before them, the Stuart monarchs believed in the Divine Right of Kings, which in simplified form meant that nobody could challenge the king's will on any matter whatsoever. In an increasingly egalitarian world the Stuarts found their divine right to rule increasingly frequently resented and challenged by

Parliament and the people. The struggle for supremacy between Parliament and the king as to who really ruled the country led to bitter civil war between the Cavaliers (Royalists) and Roundheads (Parliamentarians) of the New Model Army in 1641. The king, Charles I was eventually defeated, captured, tried, and publicly beheaded in Whitehall in 1649. For the first time Britain had an elected leader in the shape of the Puritan Oliver Cromwell who led the country through the auspices of Parliament. As Lord Protector (a title granted him in 1653) Cromwell ruled autocratically with supreme legislative and executive power. He wielded a fist of iron and all public as well as private frivolity was banned on pain of death. When he died in 1658 he was succeeded by his son, who was so unpopular that within the year Parliament, sick of years of punitive restrictions and national financial chaos, invited the son of Charles I to come back: he took the throne as Charles II in 1660. This period, known as the Restoration, brought back music and entertainment to the land; however the monarch was increasingly beholden to Parliament to grant his desires and by the time William of Orange (William III) became king, parliamentary rule was properly established. The basis of the modern political parties emerged with the Whigs and Tories. A succession of dull German kings from the house of Hannover ensued and their unpopularity in the New World lost them the American colonies after the War of Independence in 1775-83. In 1801 the legislative union of Great Britain and Ireland was implemented and the country became the United Kingdom of Great Britain and Ireland. Not long after, in 1837, a young girl of eighteen named Victoria, succeeded to the throne after her father and then uncle (William IV) died. Under her the impetus of the Industrial Revolution took Britain to the forefront of world supremacy. The British Empire was established and British Empire-builders left their homelands to explore and subjugate foreign lands. In the 1890s one person in every four on earth was a subject of Queen Victoria. During this period British society became more urban as people left the land to work in the growing cities. By the time Victoria died in 1901 Great Britain was the most powerful country in the world with an economy to match. Many British cities had their biggest growth period under her rule and much of the housing and public buildings across the land date from her era.

The global preeminence of these small islands lasted until the devastating human and economic destruction of the two World Wars. In 1921 after World War I, Ireland was partitioned into the Republic and the six northern Irish counties and the kingdom was renamed accordingly as the United Kingdom of Great Britain and Northern Ireland in 1927. In the years following, the once mighty British Empire has been dismantled— largely peacefully—with countries being given back their own destinies. Many of them chose to remain loosely affiliated through the institution of the Commonwealth.

In 1999 Scotland and Wales were both granted their own independent legislative bodies, giving them control over many areas in their respective countries. In 1953 a new Elizabethan age started with Queen Elizabeth II; the nation took new heart and slowly started to rebuild. In the last decades of the millennium the economy has slowly rebuilt and new projects and ideas are revolutionising the country. For the Millennium itself many new buildings have taken shape and new projects have been built to celebrate the new age. London itself has experienced many changes and the River Thames, so influential throughout English history, has seen a building boom to designed to make the most of her matchless beauty.

Projects for the Millennium include a Thames walkway that stretches from the Thames barrier all the way through the City of London past the green suburbs and out to Windsor and beyond. Even a short stroll along this route takes the walker through centuries of history.Intro to come from Simo

LONDON

Canary Wharf (right)

One Canada Square is London's tallest building at 800ft.

Swiss Re Building (far right)

Fosters and partners designed what has been popularly termed the "Gherkin". Finished in 2003 it is 592.1ft high.

Great Clock of Westminster (left)

Weighing 13 tons 10 cwt 3 qtr 15lb (13,760kg), the hour bell of the Great Clock of Westminster—"Big Ben"—is the most famous bell ever cast at Whitechapel.

Paternoster Square (left)

The area to the north of St. Paul's Cathedral has been extensively remodelled under the guidance of architect William Whitfield.

Royal Albert Hall (above)

The hall was conceived by Albert, Queen Victoria's beloved Prince Consort, as the centrepiece of a proposed development of a range of national institutions—cultural, scientific, and academic.

Millenium Bridge (right)

The beautiful 330ft bridge linking the Tate Modern with the north bank of the Thames was designed by Foster and Partners and opened in 2001. It closed two days after it opened because it wobbled and it would take until 27 February 2002 to rectify.

Tower Bridge (above)

Built in the Gothic style, Tower Bridge is one of the great icons of London. It was designed by architect Sir Horace Jones and the engineer John Wolfe-Barry. Work was started in 1881 and finally finished 13 years later.

Westminster Abbey (right)

A site of holy buildings since the 7th century, King William the Conqueror was crowned here on 28 December 1065 and it has been the setting for every coronation since and for numerous other royal occasions

Tower of London (far right)

Her Majesty's Tower of London was begun by William the Conqueror and added to by successive monarchs. It has been a palace, a prison, and a place of execution. The Crown Jewels are still closely guarded inside its walls.

Nelson's Column
(left)
The focal point of Trafalgar Square, the 185ft column commemorates Britain's greatest naval hero—Viscount Horatio Nelson—following his death at Trafalgar, when he defeated Napoleon's French and Spanish fleets.

Trafalgar Square
(above)
The heart of tourist London, the famous architect John Nash, designer of Regent Street, planned the first layout of the square in the 1820s, although he died before work finished.

City Hall
(right)
The new City Hall on the south bank of the Thames near Tower Bridge is home to the Mayor of London, the London Assembly, and the Greater London Authority. Designed by Fosters and Partners it opened in July 2002.

Queen Elizabeth Gate (left)
Built in 1993 for the Queen Mother, who was 93 at the time, these gates commemorate a woman taken to the nation's hearts. She died peacefully in her sleep on Saturday 30 March 2002.

Marble Arch (below)
Another Nash design, it was built in 1828 as the chief entrance to Buckingham Palace. By tradition only senior members of the royal family, the King's Troop, and the Royal Horse Artillery are allowed to ride or drive through the arch.

Tate Modern (right)
Originally the Bankside Power Station, which was designed by Sir Giles Gilbert Scott (also the architect of Battersea Power Station), the Tate Modern was converted into a gallery of modern art by the Swiss architects Herzog & de Meuron. It opened in May 2000.

Houses of Parliament
(above)

The two houses of Parliament are sited in the Palace of Westminster, once a residence of monarchs. The layout of today's building is intricate, with nearly 1,200 rooms, 100 staircases and well over two miles of passages.

Thames Barrier
(below)

Designed to protect London from flooding, work on building the barrier started in 1974. Designed by Rendel, Palmer and Tritton, it was officially opened by Queen Elizabeth II on 8 May 1984. It is 1,716ft wide and the piers are founded over 50ft below the level of the river.

St Paul's Cathedral
(right)

In AD 604, the original St Paul's Cathedral was just a small wooden church and it burned down three times before the Great Fire of London in 1666. The building we see today was designed by Britain's greatest architect—Sir Christopher Wren—and is regarded as his masterpiece.

SOUTHERN ENGLAND

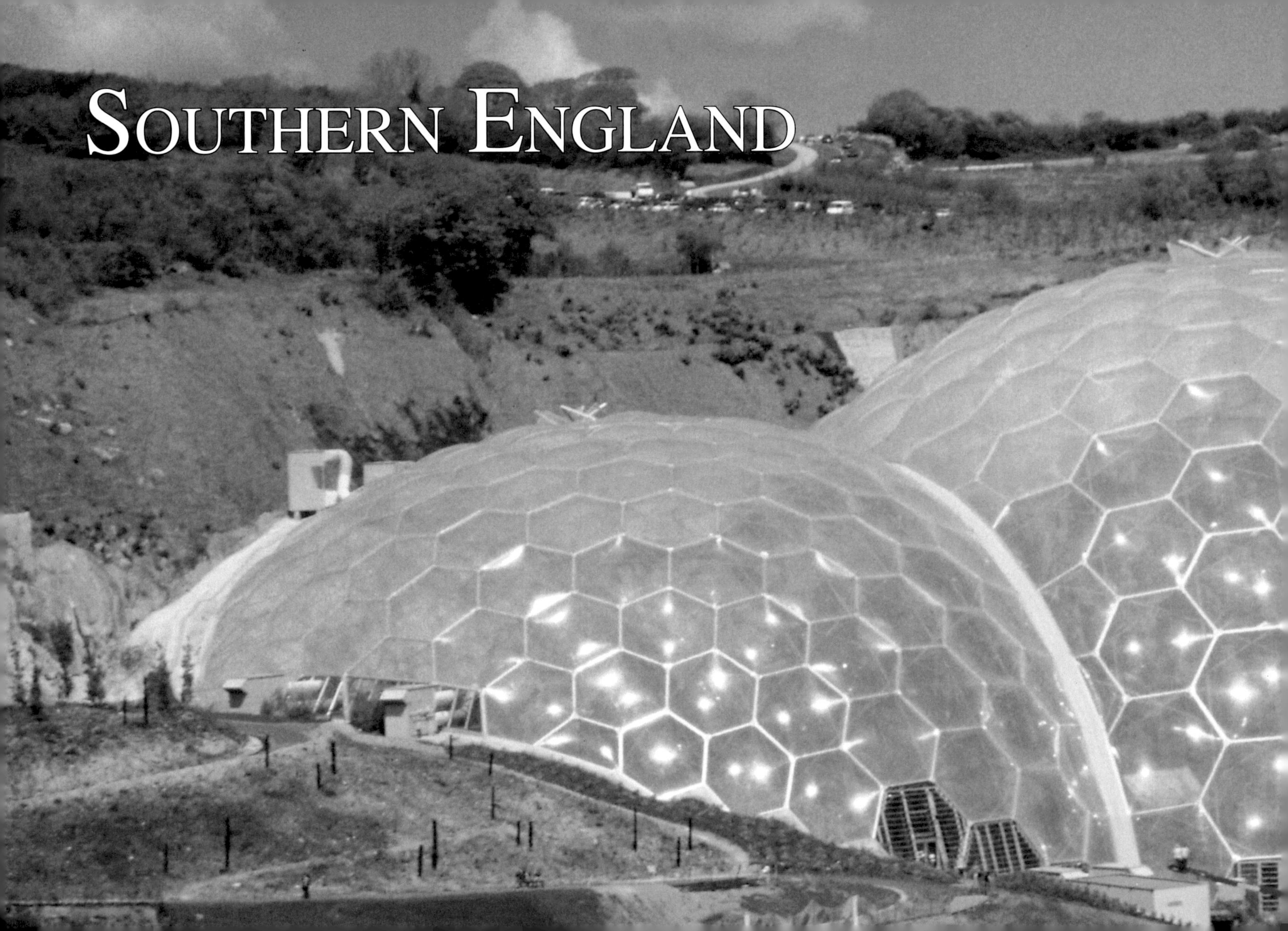

Truro
(left)
Truro Cathedral in south-west Cornwall was built from 1879) on the site of the 16th century parish church of St Mary the Virgin. The central tower and spire is 250 feet tall.

Torquay
(above)
The heart of the "English Riviera", Torquay is has been an important summer destination for tourists since the last century. It's famous inhabitants include, of course, Basil Fawlty of Fawlty Towers.

West Country coastline
(right)
The beautiful Devon and Cornwall coast has inspired many artists and writers including Agatha Christie who lived in Devon and Daphne du Maurier, who lived and wrote in Cornwall.

**Cornish Coast
(below)**
The long-distance South
West Coastal Path starts
in Dorset at South Haven
Point near Poole and runs
to Minehead in Somerset.
At 630 miles long, it is
Britain's longest national
trail.

**Pendennis Castle
(left)**
Part of the coastal defences
built by King Henry
VIII when England was
under threat of invasion
from the Continent, the
castle guards Falmouth
Bay opposite its twin, St
Mawes, on the other shore.

St Ives (right)
Cornish buildings are
traditionally built of local
granite and slate-roofed.
They need to be solidly
built to withstand
the extremes of Atlantic
weather that regularly lash
this spectacular far-
western peninsula.

St Michael's Mount (left)

Home of the St Aubyn family for 300 years since the Civil War. Separated from the mainland and the small town of Marazion by a 500-yard long natural granite causeway, when the tide is in the mount is only reachable by boat.

St Mawes Castle (above)

On one side of the River Fal guarding Falmouth Bay sits St Mawes Castle, built by Henry VIII as a small artillery fort at the same time as Pendennis Castle on the opposite shore.

Brownsea Island (right)

Brownsea Island is the largest island in Poole harbour and is owned by the National Trust. It contains a 200-acre nature reserve on the north side used by a wide range of coastal wading birds.

Brixham Harbour (left)
A replica of the Golden Hind, flagship of Sir. Francis Drake, is a living museum in Brixham harbour in south Devon. This small fishing town still depends on the sea for its livelihood.

Berry Head (above)
Twelve guns were put here during the American War of Independence, but were removed when peace came in 1783. Just ten years later, when England was yet again at war with France, guns were redeployed around the town.

Berry Head and Brixham (right)
Looking over Berry Head towards Brixham, to the right of this photograph is the breakwater of Brixham Harbour. To the left, can be seen the Mew Stone (the island), then Durl Head, and the sands of St Mary's Bay.

Torquay
(below)
Torquay is Devon's most popular tourist resort. There is a large marina and harbour at its centre—as this photograph shows.

Cockington
(right)
Two miles inland from Torquay, and accessible by a horse-drawn landau, is Cockington named after the de Cockington family who owned the manor from 1130 until 1350. A thatched village it boasts a pub designed by the famous architect Sir Edwin Lutyens, who designed the Cenotaph in London.

Torre Abbey
(right)
Near the sea front at Torquay, Torre Abbey was built in 1196 as a monastery—the ruins are still to be seen in the gardens. It became a private house after the Dissolution and was extensively rebuilt in the 18th century. The abbey is now a museum featuring a fine art display.

Royal Crescent and The Circus (left)

Bath is the best preserved Georgian city in Britain. John Wood the Elder designed the Circus which was begun in 1754. In turn his son, John Wood the Younger, designed the Royal Crescent, one of the great architectural features of a city full of spectacular buildings.

Roman Baths (above)

The Romans called Bath Aquae Sulis in honour of the spa waters found there. In the centre of the city lie the Roman Baths—among the best preserved Roman remains anywhere in England.

Pulteney Bridge (right)

English Palladian architecture at its best, Pulteney Bridge provides the perfect link between the two halves of Bath. The bridge was completed in 1773 with small shops along either side.

SS Great Britain (left)

Designed by Britain's most famous engineer, Isambard Kingdom Brunel, and built in Bristol 1843 she carried thousands of emigrants to the United States and to Australia, and acted as a troopship during the Crimean War and the Indian Mutiny.

Roman Mosaic (above)

Part of a Roman mosaic pavement dating from c. 360AD found in a newly discovered villa at Lopen, near Ilminster, Somerset, this beautiful mosaic measures almost 33ft by 20ft.

Five-Arched Railway Bridge (right)

The bridge at Creech St Michael in Somerset carried the Bristol and Exeter Railway to Chard over the River Tone. It was built in 1863 at the height of railway expansion. The line closed in 1962 and the bridge is no longer in use.

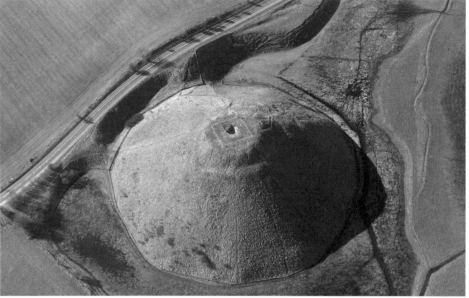

Jack the Treacle Eater Barwick Park (left)

A Grade II-listed folly dating from around 1775, the coarse rubble arch is topped with a round tower which in turn is crowned with a winged Mercury. According to local legend Jack was a local runner who carried family messages to London.

Silbury Hill (above)

The largest artificial prehistoric mound in Western Europe, Silbury Hill near Avebury is 130ft high, dates to around 2660 BC. Its purpose is a complete mystery.

Stonehenge (right)

Stonehenge is Britain's greatest prehistoric monument and a World Heritage Site. Built in three phases between 3050BC and 1600BC, it stands at the centre of a ceremonial landscape containing 450 scheduled ancient monuments of national importance.

The Needles (left)

A series of rock formations off the western point of the Isle of Wight, the Needles Lighthouse was manned until 1997.

Isle of Wight (above)

The Needles Battery on the Isle of Wight is one of many fortifications that can be found on this strategically important island. This photograph shows two 9-inch RML Mk III guns that were installed in 1873 and recovered after being rolled over the cliff when no longer required.

Longleat (right)

Regarded as the finest example of high Elizabethan architecture in Britain, Longleat was built for Sir John Thynne. The building has been extended and remodelled over the centuries; in the late 18th century "Capability" Brown landscaped the park. Today it is better known for its wildlife park.

Salisbury Cathedral (left)

The finest medieval cathedral in Britain, Salisbury was started in 1220 and completed 38 years later. Its spire, at 404ft, is the tallest in England. This view down the nave shows off the wonderful English Gothic architecture.

Harting Down (above)

211 hectares of woodland and chalk downland owned by the National Trust in West Sussex, Harting Down is traversed by the South Downs Way—a national trail and long-distance bridleway.

Radcliffe Camera (left)

The distinctive Radcliffe Camera (the word means simply "room") was built in Oxford between 1737 and 1749 with £40,000 bequeathed by Dr John Radcliffe, the royal physician, to the designs of James Gibbs.

Mottisfont Abbey Garden
(left)

Now run by the National trust, this 12th century Augustinian priory was converted into a private house after the Dissolution of the Monasteries.

Hinton Ampner Garden
(above)

One of the great gardens of the 20th century, this masterpiece of design is by Ralph Dutton, eighth and last Lord Sherborne.

Blenheim Palace and Gardens
(right)

The birthplace of Sir Winston Churchill, Blenheim Palace was built for John Churchill, the first Duke of Marlborough, and named for his great victory at Blenheim in 1704.

Mottistone Manor (left)

A fine manor house dating back to the 16th century, Mottistone Manor on the Isle of Wight, is today in the care of the National Trust. It has a renowned garden and beautiful views over the downs.

J.F. Kennedy Memorial (above)

Overlooking Runnymede, this memorial to assassinated U.S. President John F. Kennedy was unveiled by HM Queen Elizabeth II on 14 May 1965 in the presence of President Kennedy's widow and children.

Uppark (right)

Completely and meticulously restored following a fire in 1989 fire, Uppark is set high on the South Downs with magnificent views. The Georgian interior houses a collection of paintings, furniture, ceramics and an 18th-century dolls' house.

Runnymede
(left)

This attractive area
of riverside meadows,
grassland, and broadleaved
woodland, is rich in diverse
flora and fauna. It was also
the site where Magna Carta
was signed: an important
foundation stone of
modern democracy.

Petworth
(above)

A vast 17th-century
mansion set in a beautiful
park, landscaped by
'Capability' Brown and
immortalised in Turner's
paintings. Run by the
National Trust and houses
the Trust's finest and
largest collection of
pictures, by Turner, Van
Dyck, Reynolds and Blake.

The Vyne
(right)

Built in the early 16th
century for Lord Sandys,
Henry VIII's Lord
Chamberlain, the house
acquired a classical
portico in the mid-17th
century and contains a
fascinating Tudor chapel
with Renaissance glass, a
Palladian staircase, a wealth
of old panelling and fine
furniture.

Brighton Pavilion (left)

The Royal Pavilion started life as a farmhouse, but was reworked in the classical style by Henry Holland for the Prince Regent, later George IV. It was again remodelled between 1815 and 1821 into the unique building we see today by John Nash.

Firle Place (above)

Home of the Gage family for over 500 years, Firle Place in Sussex was built in the Tudor period but remodelled substantially in the 18th century. Set in wonderful parkland, it holds a fabulous collection of paintings, furniture and Sevres porcelain.

Deal Castle (right)

Commissioned by Henry VIII as part of his chain of defences against invasion by European enemies, Deal Castle is one of a number of similar forts built in the shape of the Tudor rose. When originally built the fort carried 119 guns and had a wide view along the coast and out across the Goodwins.

Winchester Cathedral (left)

The first church in Winchester was built around 650; later it became a Benedictine priory known as St Swithun's and was famous as being the final resting place for Alfred the Great in 899. The Norman cathedral was built in the 11th century and modified in the 14th.

Hever Castle (above)

Dating back to the 13th century, Hever Castle is best known as the childhood home of Henry VIII's second wife, Anne Boleyn. In 1903 it was bought by William Waldorf Astor. He spared no expense to refurbish the castle and transform its gardens.

Bodiam Castle (right)

Built in 1385 by Sir Edward Dalyngrygge, the concentric Bodiam Castle was slighted in the Civil War, when it fell to Parliamentary forces. They were ordered to dismantle it and the castle was left as a ruin until Lord Curzon bought it in 1917. He spent a fortune restoring it to the beautiful ruin it is today.

Claremont Gardens (left)

Begun in 1715 Claremont involved some of the greatest names in garden history, including Sir John Vanbrugh, Charles Bridgeman, William Kent, and "Capability" Brown.

Standen House (above)

A family house built in the 1890s, Standen was designed by Philip Webb, a friend of William Morris. A showpiece of the Arts & Crafts Movement, it is decorated throughout with Morris carpets, fabrics, and wallpapers, and contemporary paintings, tapestries, and furniture.

Canterbury Cathedral (right)

The first Gothic cathedral to be built in Britain, during medieval times it was a major centre for pilgrims, coming to pay homage at the shrine of murdered archbishop Thomas Becket.

Wisley Gardens
(above)

A very beautiful garden with romantic half-timbered Tudor-style buildings, Wisley is now run by the Royal Horticultural Society. There is a canal designed by Sir Geoffrey Jellicoe, a rock garden, formal and walled gardens by Lanning Roper, herbaceous borders, rose garden, summer garden, winter garden, and woodland garden, a fruit field, glasshouses, and an arboretum. Then there are the alpine gardens, the model vegetable gardens, and a country garden by Penelope Hobhouse.

Hampton Court
(left and right)

For almost 200 years, Hampton Court Palace was at the centre of court life, politics, and national history. Although often identified with Henry VIII, its history was influenced just as much by William III and Queen Mary II in the late 17th century. A riot of colour, the gardens of Hampton Court are always worth visiting but especially when the annual flower show takes place. Originally sponsored by Network Southeast the show was bought by the Royal Horticultural Society and has become one of the major events of the horticultural year attracting thousands.

Hatchlands, East Clandon (left)

Built in the 1750s, Hatchlands contains the earliest recorded decorations in an English country house by Robert Adam. It contains the Cobbe Collection of keyboard instruments associated with famous composers.

Ham House (above)

An outstanding Stuart house, Ham was built in 1610 and was bequeathed by the Earl of Dysart to his daughter who married the Duke of Lauderdale, a member of Charles II's influential "Cabal".

Penshurst Place (right)

The garden of Penshurst Place is the oldest in private ownership, with records dating back to the 14th century. It was a favourite of Henry VIII, who beheaded its owner and took possession of the house. His son, Edward IV, gave it to his steward, Sir William Sidney.

EAST OF ENGLAND

Kings College Chapel (left)

Henry VI was only 19 when he laid the first stone of the "College roial of Oure Lady and Seynt Nicholas" in Cambridge on Passion Sunday, 1441. Henry exercised a form of compulsory purchase and levelled houses, shops, wharves to make way for his pet project.

Peterborough (above)

There was a bronze age settlement in Peterborough 3,000 years ago. The Romans established a fortified town — Durobrivae — and the Norman's gave the city a magnificent cathedral with in which Katharine of Aragon, first wife of Henry VIII, is buried.

Cambridge (right)

Cambridge manages to combine its role as an historic city with an ancient university and, in recent years, an internationally acknowledged centre of excellence for technology and science.

Ely Cathedral (left)

Known as the "ship of the Fens", the first religious foundation at Ely was a nunnery founded in 673 AD: it was destroyed by the Danes in 869. Late in the 11th century building began on the present church which was given cathedral status in 1109.

Stratford St. Mary (above)

Stratford St Mary is the most southerly village in Suffolk and sits astride the main road to London. It boasts a magnificent church, St Mary's, and many other 15th century buildings—including the two shown here, Priest's House and Ancient House.

Lowestoft (right)

A seaside town at the most easterly point of Britain, Lowestoft has always been an important fishing port. It is also the site of Britain's first recorded lighthouse, the North Light. Benjamin Britten was born in Lowestoft in 1913.

Kersey
(left)
A picturesque Suffolk village, Kersey seems to sum up the beauties of medieval Britain with its fine half-timbered houses and the beautiful Chuch of St Mary, mentioned in Domesday Book.

Aldeburgh
(above)
The east coast of Britain is continually eroded by the sea — the Moot Hall near the sea wall was once in the centre of town — and Aldeburgh, like Dunwich to the north, was once an important port. This pretty town was the birthplace of Elizabeth Garrett Anderson in 1836.

Southwold Beach Huts
(right)
Southwold, on the Suffolk coast, is known for its church, lighthouse, newly rebuilt pier, Adnams brewery, and the seaside— as this line of beach huts testifies.

THE MIDLANDS

The Cotswolds (left)

Unarguably the most fashionable part of the area, the Cotswolds are picture-postcard lovely with golden honey-coloured stone villages all set within beautiful green rolling landscapes.

Inland waterways (above)

The heart of England is renowned for its waterways that were the arteries of the Industrial Revolution. Extensive systems linked London, Birmingham, the River Severn and the other major industrial areas: today they are mainly used for tourism.

Ironbridge (right)

The World Heritage Site of Ironbridge was the birthplace of the Industrial Revolution, where Abraham Darby pioneered the use of coke rather than charcoal in smelting iron, and where Darby's grandson, Abraham Darby III, built the world's first iron bridge in 1779.

Symonds Yat (left)

The village of Symonds Yat is divided into two separate hamlets—Symonds Yat East and West on facing banks of the River Wye. They are connected by a, man-powered rope ferry.

Symonds Yat Rock (above)

The view from Symonds Yat Rock overlooks the beautiful scenery of the Wye valley as the river twists through the gorge. Wild Peregrine falcons have long been associated with the area and RSPB telescopes are available to visitors to watch the nests during breeding season.

Great Malvern Priory (right)

Dedicated to Saints Mary and Michael and founded in 1085, the priory was rebuilt extensively in the 15th century. It has a wonderful collection of stained glass.

Ann Hathaway's Gardens (left)

Stratford-upon-Avon is synonymous with William Shakespeare. This is the thatched farmhouse that belonged to his wife Anne before she married him.

Althorp House and Park (above)

The home of the Spencer family since the early 1500s, Althorp is best known for being the final resting place of Diana, Princess of Wales.

Stanford Hall (right)

The home of the Cave family since 1430, in the 1690s the medieval house was pulled down to make way for this magnificent hall. Open to the public, Stanford houses a motorcycle museum.

**Selfridges Centre
Birmingham
(above and left)**
Opened on 4 September 2003, the redevelopment of Birmingham's Bull Ring shopping centre boasted Selfridges' new flagship department store which features a futuristic curved surface incorporating 15,000 silver-coloured spun aluminium discs.

**Brindley Place
Birmingham
(right)**
The centre of an urban regeneration project, Brindley Place is named after James Brindley, the canal pioneer. Birmingham has 180 miles of canals and 216 locks, and can claim "more canals than Venice".

Chirk Aqueduct (left)

The Llangollen Canal was opened in 1806, as spectacular as it was scenic. Of many remarkable feats of engineering, the Chirk aqueduct, designed by Thomas Telford, is the most obvious: it is 70ft high and 600ft long with 10 arches.

Stratford-upon-Avon (above)

The Bard's birthplace, his home for many years and his final resting place, there are five historic houses associated with him and his family in Stratford (see also page 70). It is also home to the Royal Shakespeare Company.

Aston Hall (right)

Built between 1618 and 1635 for Sir Thomas Holte, this fine Shropshire house is one of the last grand Jacobean houses to be built in England and has survived largely untouched by enthusiastic remodelling from later generations.

Belvoir Castle (left)

The name Belvoir meaning "beautiful view" and dates back to Norman times, when Robert de Toden built the first castle on the site. The view is still spectacular although most of the Norman castle has been superseded over the centuries.

Biddulph Grange Garden (above)

A rare and exciting survival of a High Victorian garden which contains elaborate ornamentation, Biddulph has recently been restored by the National Trust.

Canal Basin, Coventry (right)

Located on the edge of Coventry, the canal basin has fine examples of canal architecture and a 3⁄4 lifesize sculpture of famous canal engineer James Brindley, who was responsible for the initial planning of the canal navigation.

**Broadway Tower
(left and right)**
Built on an ancient beacon
site at a height of 1,000ft.
From the top on a clear
day you can see thirteen
counties. A folly designed
by James Wyatt in 1794,
it was completed around
1800.The country retreat
for the Pre-Raphaelite
artists, notably William
Morris.

**Burghley House
(above)**
Built by William Cecil
in 1587 and occupied
by his descendants ever
since, inside are 18 state
rooms filled with treasures
including art collections,
wood carvings, silver-
decorated fireplaces,
and magnificent ceilings
painted by Verrio.

Peak District (left)

It may not be as high as the Scottish Highlands, but it can certainly be as bleak. The Peak District, encompassing the Pennines between Manchester and Sheffield, was the first National Park to be set up in 1951 and covers six counties.

Chatsworth House (above)

Originally built in the 16th century, Chatsworth was rebuilt in the Classical style in the late 17th century. The 18th century saw the magnificent parkland produced by 'Capability' Brown.

Peak District (right)

Kinder Scout is a windswept plateau in the Peak District, whose highest point is Crowden Head. There are many interesting rock formations here, including this one — called the Wool Pack.

Chesterfield (left)

The crooked spire of St Mary's and All Saints Parish Church in Chesterfield is part of the identity of the town. Built in the 14th century, the spire was straight for several centuries before it began to twist: it now leans 9ft to the south and is still twisting.

Gloucester Cathedral (above)

With a history dating back to 679 AD, the building we see today was started in 1089 and continued until around 1120. The tower was added in the 15th century. More recently, the cathedral features strongly in the Harry Potter films.

Ladybower Reservoir (right)

This reservoir completely submerged the villages of Derwent and Ashopton when it was finished in 1945. One of a number of dams in the area, nearby Derwent Reservoir was used by Dr. Barnes Wallis and his team to test his bouncing bomb.

THE NORTH

Middleham Castle (left)

Although the castle was much dismantled in 1646, significant remains date back to the 1170s. Richard III acquired the castle in 1471 and his son was born here. A replica of the famous Middleham Jewel is on display.

Hawkshead Moor (above)

Set halfway between Coniston Water and Windermere near the southern edge of Esthwaite Water, the hillsides surrounding Hawkshead are part of Grizedale Forest.

Castle Howard (right)

The magnificent 18th century house was designed by John Vanbrugh and is known worldwide from its use in the television adaptation of Evelyn Waugh's *Brideshead Revisited*.

Ripon Cathedral (left)
Notable for its superb 13th century west front, 14th century stained glass, and 15th century wood carvings, Ripon Cathedral was greatly restored in the 19th century.

Scarborough Castle (above)
Scarborough Castle is sited on the remains of a 4th century Roman signal station on a headland above the town. The castle dates from the 12th century.

Conisbrough Castle (right)
The ruins of a Norman stronghold on top of Saxon defences, the romantic appeal of Conisbrough Castle was not lost on Sir Walter Scott who used the tiny third floor chapel as the setting for a scene in his great romantic novel *Ivanhoe*.

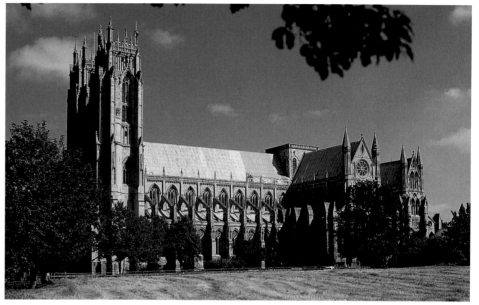

Richmond Castle (left)

The imposing remains of Richmond Castle tower over the River Swale in North Yorkshire. Between c.1080 and 1170, the keep was once 100ft high and one of the finest in the country.

Beverley Minster (above)

The Church of St John the Evangelist, Beverley Minster is on the site of a Saxon church and is the most splendid collegiate church in the country. It is built in Medieval Gothic architecture of the English Perpendicular style.

Selby Abbey (right)

Dating back to 1069, Selby Abbey was built in late Norman and Early English styles. It is a magnificent example of a monastic abbey finding a new purpose as a parish church.

Brontë Parsonage (left)

The house in Haworth was built in 1778 and now belongs to the Brontë Society. The Brontës were an extraordinary family, Charlotte, Emily, and Anne wrote, *Jane Eyre, Wuthering Heights,* and *The Tenant of Wildfell Hall*.

Beningbrough Hall (above)

This handsome Queen Anne house was built in 1716. The Hall contains 100 portraits of the period 1688-1760 on loan from the National Portrait Gallery, and a Victorian laundry showing 19th century domestic life.

Harewood House (right)

Designed by John Carr in 1759 for Edwin Lascelles, Harewood House in Leeds has been lived in by his family ever since. In 1772 "Capability" Brown started work on the surrounding park.

Shibden Hall (left)

Dating originally from around 1420, Halifax's Shibden Hall is a distinctive half-timbered house with later additions. It has period rooms furnished in the styles of the 17th, 18th, and 19th century.

Victoria Centre & Gardens, Harrogate (above)

Harrogate has all the old-fashioned dignity of a popular spa town and has long been a favourite place for "taking the waters".

Student Union Building, Sheffield (right)

The former National Centre for Pop Music is now owned by Sheffield Hallam University. The modern, aluminium-panelled building was designed by architects Branson Coates.

Humber Bridge (left)

Completed in 1981, at 6,660ft the Humber Bridge is the longest single-span suspension bridge in the world. Making it involved over 71,000km of wire and took eight years; it was opened officially by the Queen on 17 July 1981.

The Royal Armouries Museum (above)

Housing 3,000 years of military history and over 8,000 spectacular exhibits, the Royal Armouries Museum in Leeds has the first tiltyard built in Britain in 400 years.

Lake Gormire (right)

Created by a landslip during the Ice Age, Lake Gormire is one of only two natural lakes in Yorkshire. It can be seen from the Cleveland Way which runs for 109 miles from Helmsley to Filey south of Scarborough.

Viaduct on the River Nidd (left)

Carrying local trains between York and Leeds via Knaresborough, the viaduct has already fallen down twice. The local 16th century witch Mother Shipton prophesied that if it fell down a third time the world would end!

Runswick Bay (above)

Lying about five miles north of Whitby, Runswick is split into two parts—a few houses at the top of the cliffs contrast sharply with the red-roofed cottages that tumble down the cliffside to the seafront below.

Thornwick Bay (right)

Thornwick Bay is one of the inlets on the north side of Flamborough Head, a rocky chalk headland jutting out into the North Sea on the Yorkshire coast.

Hallith Wood (left)

A 15th century building on the northern fringes of Bolton, Lancashire — Hall ith Wood dates back to 1483 — this was the home of Samuel Crompton who invented his Spinning Mule in this building. In memory of this Hall ith Wood has been a textile museum since 1902.

Lancaster Canal (above)

Construction began in 1792 on a 75-mile long canal from Westhoughton, east of Wigan, to Kendal. It was never completed, although sections were built from Clayton to Chorley, Preston to Kendal and a branch to Glasson Dock near Lancaster.

Lyme Park Hall (right)

The home of the Legh family for 600 years, Lyme was transformed from a Tudor country house by the Venetian architect Leoni into an Italianate palace. It is best known as the setting for the BBC's *Pride and Prejudice*.

Salford Quays, Manchester (left and right)

The Manchester Ship Canal allowed ocean-going vessels to reach docks close to the centre of Manchester—the main docks were at Salford. However, the development of container ports and motorway links outweighed the convenience of ships being able to reach Manchester and in the 1980s most of the docks were closed. Salford docks have now been redeveloped as Salford Quays. These photos show the Quay House public house (left) and the Victoria Harbour Building (right).

Smithills Hall, Bolton (above)

One of the oldest manor houses in Lancashire, with parts dating from the 14th century and a great hall built in the 15th century, Smithills Hall is presently being restored to become a Heritage Centre.

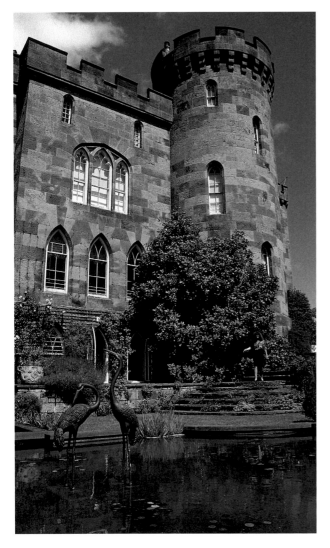

Cholmondeley Castle (left)

Cholmondeley, near Malpas in Cheshire is home to a family that came to England with the Norman Conquest. Around 1700, Hugh Cholmondeley rebuilt the mansion and laid out magnificent formal gardens.

Buxton (above)

The highest town in Britain, Buxton is known for its waters and is second only to Bath as a spa. Set in the middle of the beautiful countryside just outside the Peak District National Park, Buxton lies on the River Wye.

Tatton Park (right)

Now owned by the National Trust, Tatton Park, Cheshire, was built in the late 18th/ early 19th century for William Egerton by Samuel and Lewis Wyatt. The magnificent gardens include 54 acres landscaped by Humphrey Repton.

Rievaulx Abbey (left)
Founded by the Cistercians in 1131 in a remote part of North Yorkshire, Rievaulx rapidly grew and soon was home to 140 monks and 500 lay brothers. It was largely destroyed in 1539 during the Dissolution of the Monasteries.

Foxdenton Hall (above)
The house dates back to the early 1400s, but it was rebuilt in the 17th century and then at the turn of the 18th into the form seen today.

Lancashire Moorland (right)
The northwest of England contrasts wonderful, bleak moorland against areas of conurbation that built up around the major industries of Lancashire—coal, cotton, and shipping.

Bramall Hall
(left)

The oldest parts of Bramall Hall in Cheshire date from the 14th century. It is one of the county's best-preserved black and white timber-framed buildings.

Leighton Hall
(above)

Set in beautiful parkland against a backdrop of the Lakeland Fells, the neo-Gothic Leighton Hall in Carnforth, Lancashire, is thehome of the famous furniture making Gillow dynasty.

Stapeley Water Gardens
(right)

Just outside Nantwich in Cheshire, this large nursery specialises in water plants and attracts 1.5 million visitors each year. It is the home of the National Collection of Nymphae and over 350 varieties of waterlily are grown here.

Angel of the North (left)

Love it or hate it, Antony Gormley's steel sculpture cannot be ignored! Higher than four double-deck buses; almost as wide as the wingspan of a Jumbo jet, it greets visitors as they reach Gateshead, by the A1 or East Coast main line.

Yorkshire Coast (above)

The northeast coast of Britain is spectacularly beautiful — from the gentle charms of Filey and Scarborough to the bleak beauty of Northumbria.

Tyne Bridge (right)

One of the great icons of northern England, when the Tyne Bridge between Newcastle and Gateshead was finished in 1928 it was the largest single span in the world.

H.M. Bark Endeavour (left)

James Cook was born in Yorkshire on October 27, 1728 and undertook his first voyage of exploration in the Endeavour in 1769 to examine the transit of Venus across the face of the Sun. He would die on his third voyage in the Hawaiian Islands on February 14, 1779.

Alnwick Castle (above)

A magnificent border fortress dating back to the 11th century, Alnwick was extensively restored by Robert Adam in the mid-19th century.

Warkworth Castle (right)

Warkworth Castle was the home of the Percys, a great Catholic family that lost its position under Queen Elizabeth. The castle fell into disrepair in the late 17th century and only these beautiful ruins remain.

Tynemouth Castle (left)

Tynemouth was originally a priory and the burial place of the kings of Northumbria. Destroyed by the Danes in 865 AD, it was refounded as a Benedictine Priory. Fortified in the 13th century, it is now a picturesque ruin.

Bamburgh Castle (above)

This stunning coastal site has been occupied with a fortress since the Iron Age. The present 11th century castle was a Norman stronghold which survived many sieges and welcomed many English kings as guests.

Lindisfarne, Holy Island (right)

Built in 1550 using stones taken from Lindisfarne Priory, the castle was converted into a magnificent private home by the architect Sir Edwin Lutyens in 1903. The island is now a wildlife sanctuary.

Durham Cathedral (left)
Built in the late 11th and early 12th centuries to house the relics of St Cuthbert and the Venerable Bede, the cathedral is the largest and best example of Norman-style architecture in England.

Cannon Hall (above)
Set in 70 acres of parkland and gardens, Cannon Hall in Barnsley opened as a museum in 1957 and contains collections of furniture, paintings, glassware and pottery, as well as the Regimental Museum of the 13th/18th Hussars.

Cumbria (right)
The Lake District is as beautiful a place as any in Britain, contrasting the lush green of the valleys and lakesides with the harshness of stone crags and fells.

Lake District (left)

Looking towards the Langdale Pikes from Blea Tarn, the very heart of wild Lakeland, between Great Langdale and Little Langdale.

Hardknott Fort (above)

Called Mediobogdum by the Romans and built between 120 and 138AD, Hardknott controlled the famous pass of the same name on the road from Ravenglass (Glannaventa) on the west coast to Ambleside (Galava).

Derwentwater (right)

Keswick is the chief town of the North Lake District and is beautifully situated near the north shore of Lake Derwentwater between the towering hills of Skiddaw and Saddleback.

Lough Rigg Fell (left)

1,099 feet above Ambleside in the Lake district, there's a wonderful panorama from the top of Lough Rigg Fell from where you can see the Langdale Pikes and across to the Fairfield Horseshoe.

Helvellyn (above)

One of the highest fells in the Lake District at 3,118ft, the most spectacular ascent of Helvellyn is via Striding Edge. Many famous visitors have made this demanding climb including William Wordsworth and Sir Walter Scott.

Side Pike (right)

On the southern side of Langdale is Lingmoor Fell and Side Pike, from where there are excellent views of the more-frequented Langdale Pikes, which dominate the northern side of this beautiful valley.

Cat Bells (left)

View of Cats Bells near Keswick in the Lake District. From the top there are fantastic views of Borrowdale, Derwentwater, Blencathra, Latrigg, Skiddaw and Bassenthwaite Lake.

Bassenthwaite (above)

Bassenthwaite Lake, owned by the National Park Authority, is one of the largest at 4 miles long and 3/4 mile wide, but also one of the shallowest (70 ft). It is the most northerly of the lakes, and has no major settlements on its shores.

Wast Water (right)

The rugged and isolated Wasdale valley and its lake were formed by glaciation. At three miles in length and a half mile in width, Wast Water is England's deepest lake, reaching downward 258 feet.

**York Minster
(left and above)**

From Roman times to the present day the site on which
York Minster stands has been at the very centre of
England's religious and political life. The present Minster
was built between the 12th and the 15th centuries and is
the largest Gothic church in England. The Foundations
Museum under the Minster shows how the present
building was constructed on the site of a Norman
Cathedral, which was itself built on a Roman Fort.